Praises
and
Ponderings
from a
Poet's Path

Megan E. Vance

Copyright © 2019 Megan E. Vance

All rights reserved. This book or any portion thereof may not be reproduced, performed or used in any manner whatsoever without the express written permission of the publisher or author except for the use of brief quotations in a book review.

Printed in the United States of America

First Printing 2019

ISBN 13: 978-1-948894-06-7

Tree Shadow Press

www.treeshadowpress.com

For reproduction permission, contact:

treeshadowpress@gmail.com

DEDICATION

I dedicate this book to the Dread Champion,
my Lord and Savior Jesus Christ.

"But the LORD is with me like a dread champion;
Therefore, my persecutors will stumble and not prevail."
Jeremiah 20:11a (*NASB*)

"For from Him and through Him and to Him are all things.
To Him be the glory forever. Amen."
Romans 11:36 (*NASB*)

CONTENTS

CHRISTMAS PONDERINGS

Have I Room for Jesus?	1
Trade Heartbreak for HIM	2
One Look	3
You Were Meant for More	4
Christmas, 1985	6
While Creatures Gaze	8

PRAISE PONDERINGS

Nothing You Can Do	11
Dying is Living	12
God Knows	14
Infinity	15
Give Thanks	16
Jesus is Faithful	18
Biding Time	19
Whosoever Will	20
Hidden in God	22
To Be His Friend	23
Face to Face	24
My Failure, His Favor	25
The Girl on the Bottom Rung	26
Look and See	27
Dead Men Walking	28
The One Desire	29

PEOPLE PONDERINGS

Prayer for New Grandson	33
Still Blessed to Hold her Hand	34
Old Man in a Wheelchair	36
Waiting for the Son	39
Peter and Eli	40
For J.P.	41

Rip and Re-Sew	42
Give Me Some Blue	44
My Father's New Suit	46
Just Who?	47
Old Feet	48

POTPOURRI OF PONDERINGS

The Wandering Lamb	53
Harmar Eagle	54
Hardened to Wonder	56
Post-It Note to Self	57
Let Go the Chain	58
Redeeming Time	59
How Could it Be?	60
Look Up	61
Creation is Crying	62
Particles	63
Sudden Change	64
On Being Broken	65
Turn Me	66
When Confusion Comes In	68
My Work	69
Don't We All Need Jesus?	70
Still	71
ABOUT THE AUTHOR	72

ACKNOWLEDGMENTS

My gratitude to my loving husband Kevin for helping me with all computer issues and constantly cheering me on. Thank you to my dear mother Nancy Murphy, who always encourages me in my writing.

Thank you to all writing friends (you know who you are) who helped weed out redundancies and passive words in early drafts of my poetry.

Thank you to my sister Claire Knolle for help and advice when this project was just getting started.

Finally, to my publisher, friend, fellow writer and poet Deb Sanchez from Tree Shadow Press: a great big thank you for your willingness to publish this collection of heartfelt poetic musings.

I am blessed.

CHRISTMAS

PONDERINGS

Nativity Scene drawn by the author in her college days.

Have I Room for Jesus?

No room for the Babe in Bethlehem's inn,
I ask, is their room in my heart?
No place to lay the Lamb's sweet head,
From very beginning, they wanted Him dead.

Have I made welcome God's Risen Son?
Is He presently living through me?
Or have I cast grace and mercy aside,
Subtly siding with the wicked one's lie?

The Lamb is now a Mighty Lion
Waiting for word to descend for His kids.
He'll restore what's broken and make things right
All of mankind will bow down in His sight.

Oh, if His enemies could only make room,
Take offer of rescue from eternal doom.
For the King of Kings and Lord of Lords,
Simple faith is what He rewards.

Trade Heartbreak for HIM

If as you look around you
Find this world to be a lie
And all the heartbreak makes no sense
Each day ending with a sigh.

If you've found your heart's grown numb
To hatred and corruption deep
And you can only hang your head
Even mourning in your sleep.

Then I say: "There's yet good news!"
You are here for something higher
Than simply to groan through each day
A greater purpose for you to aspire.

He put you here to know Him well
Enjoy His friendship every day
Receive by faith His sacred claim
Trust His love has made a way.

Glory to God in all the highest
And peace to those who share His favor
Take His gift of righteousness
Find faith, hope, love now yours to savor.

One Look

If all the needs
Of a desperate world
Were boiled down to one
Then every creature
Born alive
Need gaze upon the Son.

There is no peace
Without Jesus
But with Him there is light
Enough to fill the darkest heart
To light the blackest night.

Don't fool yourself
For no cheap trinket
Of Planet Earth could satisfy
They charm and sparkle
Like fine champagne
But in the end, they lie.

Just take one look
At Jesus, see
How beautiful His face
Receive His gift
Eternal life
And enjoy His endless grace.

You Were Meant for More

It's almost time for Christmas
And you know what *that* means
It's time to fill our bellies
And decorate with greens.

It's almost time for Christmas
But does your heart despair?
There is no peace on earth now
Does anybody care?

Our world indeed has gone insane
In longing yearns to fill its being
True joy escaping most of us
All satisfaction fleeing.

"As long as *I* have what *I* need
No need to think of others
God did not surely mean
That I'm the keeper of my brother."

No wonder then, at Christmas
So many take their lives
As they struggle to find meaning
The Lord they cannot recognize.

The Babe that came so long ago
He longs to take your pain
If you will simply trust in Him
And rely upon His name.

To each soul now He whispers
"Do you believe in Me?
My ways are not like others
I came to set you free."

Peace then, in a Person.
Not wrapped up in a bow
He came to give His life to us
His grace and love to show.

Christmas, 1985

I often think of Christmas
As gifts around a tree
But the best gift of Christmas
Was from God Himself to me.

As we unwrap our presents
We are happy to receive
But something deep is missing
Until we just believe.

Christmas is not presents
Nor Santa Claus, nor bows
Nor shopping sprees, nor parties
No, Christmas is not those.

Christmas is but one gift;
A gift from God to man
It's free to every person
Who believes in God's plan.

"For God so loved the world
That He sent His only Son,"
By trusting that He died for you
Your salvation can be won.

The Bible says we all have sinned
And come short of God's glory
Admit that you're a sinner
And believe the Christmas story.

Why did Jesus come to earth?
He came to die on a cross
Not to prophesy or do good deeds
He came to save the lost.

So, that is why the Christ was born
So many years ago
He came for you, oh friend of mine
It's <u>you</u> He wants to know.

While Creatures Gaze

While creatures gaze into the skies
They long with hope for peace on earth
They know it will not come from here
But a world beyond where Love resides.

Love came down and stayed to give
To pay redemption sacrifice
And all the while Love did, He shared
Gave us Words on which to live.

Love told us He would come again
As we watch, creation groans
With every shake and every storm
Enemy knows his times at end.

Love will come and set things right
The King all glorious above
Lamb and lion shall lie together
True peace for Love came down that night.

PRAISE

PONDERINGS

Modern baptismal site on the Krenides Stream, Philippi, Greece. Taken by the author October 2008.

Nothing You Can Do

There is nothing you can do today
To make God love you more.
His love is as high as the stars in the sky
As deep as the ocean floor.

Don't I have to do good deeds?
One perplexed will say to me
But our good deed is to believe in Him
Just be who He made you to be.

You are free then to love Him, free to serve
All by His undeserved grace
Do you see His hand outstretched to you?
On the cross He took your place.

Jesus loves me, this I know
The sweetest words ever said.
Just get to know His love for you
Let His word be your daily bread.

Dying is Living

I could sit here and mutter
I could sit here and gripe
About all "injustices"
Dark times in my life.

But it's so much better
To trust in the Lord.
Believe His great love
Will bestow full reward.

So much easier and kinder,
To stay with my Christ.
Than to face barren desert
Outside with no life.

Sweet praise flows to Jesus,
Savior and Friend.
To Him be the Glory
From now 'til the end.

The end of myself, too.
For you see, I have died.
As Jesus hung dying,
I, too crucified.

To be free from self's tyranny
Indeed, adds no sorrow.
And will help me ensure
A most lovely tomorrow.

It seems a paradox
For to die is to live
And to take from the Giver
All the grace He can give.

God Knows

God knows we all have heartache
God knows we all have grief
In bearing senseless tragedy
During a fleeting life so brief.

How is it that He knew them all?
Knew them before time began
And if we simply trust in Him
He'll work them for good in His plan.

For God keeps every tear we cry
And it pains Him in His heart
He mines out diamonds from our trials
The richest blessings to impart.

Infinity

A grain of salt in endless shaker
Yet I am blessed to know my Maker
A bubble in depthless, churning sea
Yet known to Him from eternity
How is it my dear Lord and God
Came to share this shattered sod
Infinite love, ceaseless dose poured
On those who cursed, whipped, abhorred
Our Jesus, sinless Son of Man
Still He includes me in His plan
God's way is grace, His work is finished
Christ's mercy will not be diminished
Dear friend will you reach and take Him too?
For Jesus Christ is calling you
"Today," He says, "Will you hear My voice?"
Just make one simple, solemn choice
Upon His blessed name believe
Christ's own righteousness you'll receive.

Give Thanks

Birds are singing their praises
In varied melodies
Giving credence, praises to their Creator,
Without knowing what they do –
Or do they?

Maybe the animals have
More sense than men.
Know without shadow of doubt
They have a Creator
Magnificent, all powerful,
All knowing,
Who made each one.

Our feathered friends say, "Thank You"
In trills, chirps, calls,
Even caws.
Each one remembers to say
Thank You to Him who made them.

We humans forget to say thank You.
And that's when it all goes wrong.
First step off the track
Of the heavenly highway
Is to refuse to give Him thanks.
For He is in control of all things:
Yes, even things we cannot figure out.

Yet if I stop and pause
To give Him thanks,
It will prove that I do believe
In what He promised:
All things – the good, the awful,
The gut-wrenching,
The confusing,
Allowed by Him for my ultimate good.

If I love Him,
Then He declares that this is true.
Showers of blessing
Through all the storms of life
To that child who believes without seeing
And gives thanks unto His name.

Jesus is Faithful

Jesus is faithful
Though I'm filled with confusion
Jesus is faithful
Though bombarded by lies
Jesus is faithful
Though other's tongues cut like knives
Jesus is faithful
Though the devil assails me
Jesus is faithful
And He cannot but be so
When I want to give up
My Jesus is faithful.

Biding Time

I will trust You for today, Lord,
Even though I seem a fool.
I will lean upon Your holy Name,
On highest throne You rule.

I will trust You for today, Lord,
Though my mind wants to rebel.
To whom else could I go but You?
You are faithful – I will tell.

Through suffering we a Kingdom gain,
And by faith we will endure.
In His mind it's already done.
Our destiny's secure.

What reunion there will be,
Arriving on the other side.
I will trust You for today, Lord,
Time's "little while" to bide.

Whosoever Will

He endured thick darkness
Suffering and shame.
He endured thick darkness
To take away my blame.

His body fully broken
Great drops of blood outpoured,
To take the fearsome penalty
And wrath of God's own sword.

And yet during time of judgment,
He thoughts were still on me.
What kind of love is this to men?
Planned from eternity.

From beginning of creation,
Redemption was His thought.
Kindness, grace, and mercy:
The only things He sought.

And so now we can seek Him,
No matter what our state.
Though we've run from Jesus' love,
It's not yet too late.

While we still are breathing
His offer is extended
For our sin has been wiped away
To Him, our judgment's ended.

The cup of our salvation
God will now pour out and fill.
Heaven's gates are standing open
For whosoever will.

Hidden in God

I rest my case with You Lord.
Right or wrong? I don't know,
Conscience accusing repeatedly.
Am I mistaken, or correct?
Does it even matter?

I don't know, but I rest my case with You
You judge me, Lord,
For Your judgments are faithful.
It doesn't matter if I'm right,
Just let me hide myself in You.

In the cleft of the Rock you'll find me
For judgment has passed by.
The ledger has been cleared.
Because of the kindness of Another,
I am hidden with Christ in God.

To Be His Friend

If the wind and sea obeyed You, Lord,
It shouldn't be hard for me.
The enemy whispers it's just too much,
And desires my misery.

Hoarding and saving my life will cause
Loss of it in the end.
When I obey I'll save my life,
For I want to be called His friend.

Face to Face

Jesus bids me come to Him,
Not cower in disgrace.
Because His victory tore the veil,
I see Him face to face.

He longs for me to fully know,
That He has done it all.
His justice breached an infinite gap
The curse which came from Adam's fall.

Jesus longs to see me come
He's never too busy for me.
A personal audience with the King of Kings.
To present my every plea.

What cost came for the Son of Man
To make this New and Living way?
I can only give Him thanks
Yet cannot ever repay.

My Failure, His Favor

Silence in my soul
Battered holes within my heart.
Where are You, God?
Don't You see the pain in my soul?
Hear me as I keep crying to You.

There are no earthly comforts.
I am embarrassed of who I am.
And fear prickles its way inside too.
Fear that I will be ashamed, not able to stand.
Where are You, God?

Why have You turned Your back on me?
If I could sum up my life, in one word
Failure it would be.
Total and complete failure.
Where are You Jesus?

My heart cannot bear the pain.
But then I remember,
You tell me, when I am weak,
Then You can be strong in me.
Failure, it plunges me ever towards You.

Failure makes me run
Into Your streams of mercy
And undeserved kindness.
Today and forever, I will trade my failure
For Your oceans of gracious favor.

The Girl on the Bottom Rung

What should I say today?
That I have made it up the ladder of success?
No, I think not.
I didn't make it up there, you see.
Somehow, I got stuck on the bottom rung
Kind of got hung up there.
I was waiting there on the bottom rung for my life to begin.

It is a paradox; I hope you know
What we see around us, it's an illusion.
Nothing is as it seems.
Material world and popularity
Passing by, slowly fading away: *Sit transit Gloria mundi*.
What is alive now will soon be dead
There is another world we perceive only by faith.
The first are last, and the last are first.

Lord, open my eyes to this world of faith.
You are not against me
Your love is as high as the heavens
Could it really be that much?
You said it, so it must be true.
Guess I will think on that for a lifetime.
Your love overflowing to the girl on the bottom rung.

Look and See

If you're lonely there's One
Who's waiting to hear
If your heart lies wounded
He is near you, so near!

Waiting, He pauses
Until we give in
And admit that we've wandered
By our guilt and our sin.

He knows we can't do it
Despite our best plan
Still the Father is waiting
To be gracious to man.

A plan inconceivable
He made long ago
Despite all our cruelty
And lives filled with woe.

God's plan from the start
Only Son would He send.
He's waiting for any who
Will take Him as friend.

Sent as an offering
For you and for me
Stare fully at Jesus
And at last you will see.

Dead Men Walking

We were born like Lazarus,
In deeds and sins were dead.
It would have always been that way
Had not our Savior bled.

We are all named Lazarus,
And risen from the dead.
When we in Christ alone believe
He's now our rightful head.

For we're all dead men walking,
Dead in sins or to the cry,
Of him who wants to raise his voice
Against the Lord Most High.

But since we cannot lift a finger
To change our hopeless condition.
We get to look away from self
And learn of our new position.

The old grand story is still new,
Sinners Christ died to save.
He paid the penalty for us all
And triumphed over the grave.

And we too, if found in Him,
Will live forevermore.
As we wait expectantly
For the Kingdom He'll restore.

The One Desire

I live in a time where there's too many choices,
Surrounded, ensnared, by too many voices.
Clamoring, demanding all my attention,
With each day, I lose a bit more retention.
What does the future hold, how should I then live?
To whom should I all my energy give?

A time of great grief, overwhelming sorrow,
And yet I must face the day called tomorrow.
For it has not appeared what yet I will be,
But when Jesus returns, His face I shall see.
And all the learned ones, great books and media,
Will confess that Jesus is God's cyclopedia.

For every atom came forth from His hand,
And nothing did happen without His command.
All libraries everywhere upon this sphere,
Could never contain the One we hold dear.
And His essence is love, of that we are sure,
Because of the cross He chose to endure.

Life as we know it will from earth disappear,
My jaded pursuits will finally be clear.
"It wasn't important," He'll whisper to me,
"For I was the One thing that mattered, truly
I always loved you and was always enough.
You didn't need people; you didn't need stuff."

I'll bow down before Him, His eyes flames of fire,
And in one moment know He was all my desire.

PEOPLE

PONDERINGS

Above Left: Mom, Nancy Elizabeth Creasy, in 1948, Aspinwall PA

Above Right: Dad: John Claire Murphy in 1949, Jefferson IA

Below: Mom and Dad's wedding, June 21, 1958

Prayer for New Grandson

As she struggles to bring forth
The cycle of life continues onward
Give her strength just now
Oh God of every kind of grace.

We had our time – it is now theirs
The mantle of life to carry on
Sharing in human procreation,
And life marches on.

Bring the child to this world
Without so much travail.
Bless with spiritual blessings the life
That is ready to spring forth.

God our Father, You are the Giver
Please blow Your breath of life.
And when the right time comes
Give him eternal life as well.

A man loves a woman
And in return, she rewards his love,
Bearing life to carry on his name.
My son – a father now

Because of love
Because of Your life.

Still Blessed to Hold her Hand

I place my middle-aged hand
On top of her tiny withered one
As we sang hymns together
In church today.
And it hit me suddenly
One day
I will no longer hear her singing along.
Never again shall I
hear her recite the Lord's Prayer
After all these years.
A strong dose of reality hit me
Calloused and blinded as I am.
Treasure her, a little voice inside me said.

She won't be here forever.
Well, of course I know that.
But then again, my mother.
Not someone else's, but mine.
The one who held my hand
So long ago,
The one who wiped away my tears.

She wasn't a perfect mother.
God knows, neither was I.
We haven't always
Seen eye to eye either.
She is precious nonetheless
Little wilted woman
Who longs for God to take her.

She needs me and
God says never to despise her
When she is old.
That's enough for me.

Middle aged hand over old hand
As young mother hand of days past
once clasped chubby toddler hand,
Hands that held me from danger, or
Folded in prayer to plead for me.
Her heart anxious when I made
A stupid choice,
Or wrecked the car,
Or had a nervous breakdown.

She is wearing weary of this world.
And I am next in line.

Mom, I don't deride you
Though sometimes things get hard.
And life gets messy.
We're too alike, we've always said.
Mom? She still can hear me.

I am glad that I still have the chance
To tell you that I love you
Still feel the warmth of life
Still blessed to hold your hand.

Old Man in a Wheelchair

Old Al was bald
Decked in flannel pajama pants and worn black slippers
Confined to a wheelchair.
An Air Force veteran, no less,
Observed by his wearing bold blue and white
USAF lanyard around his neck.

Widower that he was,
Al seemed friendly to my also widowed mom.
One night he wheeled over
Across the hall
Brought her "cheer" in a fuzzy navel
Libation from within
A red plastic cup.
"Now that'll putcha ta sleep!"
He chuckled before wheeling back
Across the hall.

I talked to him
About his life, his wife,
His daughters
And time in the Air Force.
How he'd barely escaped the Korean War.

One cold winter day
He appeared again at the door
Of Mom's room.
In his trembling hand he
Held a tray of cupcakes.

"It's my birthday," he said.
"Have a cupcake with me."
So, we did.
Sweet old Al.

Next time I saw him
Al was coughing.
"Not goin' ta lunch, I'm sick," he said.
Then he was gone.
Off to the hospital,
They said.
Never strong enough
To return again
to his room across the hall.

Yesterday I scrolled through
Death notices.
To my surprise

There, with cheerful face,
(And Air Force lanyard still round his neck.)
Was a photo of Al,
No longer of this world.

Suddenly, I remembered
The cupcakes, the trembling hands
His last birthday.
(And how I pushed down the thought
That it could be his last.)

Dear Al,
Just an old man in a wheelchair.
I only knew him
For a brief little space of time.
One dot on a line
Spreading out to eternity.

His life mattered,
Yes, it did.
I hope I see him again
At the grand reunion in the sky.
No more fuzzy navels needed
Something better awaits us.

Waiting for the Son

I'm waiting on a transport chair
Mom's forgetting how to walk.
The one comprising all my world,
Who was my steady rock.

She forgets to wipe her face,
Her speech of minutes ago.
Death approaches creep by creep,
Her shuffling movements slow.

It hurts for me to watch as
She's living with no joy.
Oblivious to all God's gifts,
Except grand-girl and boys.

They will come to visit today,
Her sorrow eased but a little while.
Til her Heavenly Friend takes her home,
Her longing eased when she sees His smile.

My Mom was all the world to me,
She is now my little one.
Depending daily for my help,
Waiting at last to see the Son.

Peter and Eli

Peter and Eli
Are the best of friends.
May it be that way
When they've grown to be men.

Peter and Eli
With their bright blue eyes,
Inherited from Mama
May they grow to be wise.

Peter and Eli
Are just little boys
Roll tractors on carpet
And have simple joys.

Peter and Eli
My grandsons, you see.
I pray for their future
And eternity.

Two precious brothers
Give us joy and delight.
They'll soon be adults
May they walk in His might.

I pray for these little ones,
And their cousin J.P.,
May they all know His love,
And fine men grow to be.

For J.P.

How many days
Has grandbaby to play?
Don't make him hurry,
To learn the world's way.
Let him see the wonder,
Let him feel loved.
Let him sense the magic,
Without push and shove.
No rush to grow up,
To find out the world's pain.
Let him think all is well,
Let him play in the rain.
He is well-loved, and time will tell
The man he will be.
Let him grow up slowly
Let his little eyes see
The wonder of God's world.

Let him be J.P.

Rip and Re-Sew

Cutting out squares and rectangles
ripping and re-sewing
linking fabrics together
not random, painstakingly
row by row
some rows weren't quite even
even as her life wasn't.
Still, she created cloth tapestry
combining colors
of golds, pinks and yellow
not to mention faded green with dots
tints of grace
were added that still made life sweet.
Feline fabrics showed her affections
toward furry friends
she knew once and loved.
In memories of days,
months and years
she marveled how time had arranged
fleeting filaments of
her life's own tapestry
now, nearly hemmed to completion.
Yet, some mistakes remained
stubbornly stitched
despite attempts
to rip and re-sew
tacitly, they remained
tacked and tied together.

Knowing she could not return, or
re-stitch story once again
at least she
joyed at chance
to craft something pretty,
not perfect,
but yet something new.
And all the while
she kept on praying
that her life seams imperfectly sewn
would disentangle, somehow.
One day she awakened,
gazed and gasped
Her God had tailored stubborn seams
to exactly suit her patch-worked life story.
Smiling, she placed that time-worn needle
on table
to rest with her at last.

Give Me Some Blue

"Give me some blue," my father said,
Startling me from deep teenage slumber.
I opened green-blue eyes—not to see the blessings,
But in a grumbledy-funk sort of thankless way.
Most reluctantly I rose from
Security of warm blankets,
Off to face another dreary day of school.

Mama tread, tiny feet on eggshells, upstairs with my coffee,
Tailor made for me, but did I thank her?
No, I did not, as she reminded me later,
Just a few snarls here and there.
Probably to argue with my sister,
Who would hit the shower first, as we all scrambled, quarreling,
To be on time for the blasted bus.

Born on the last day of winter, I was.
(Thinking to grumble on that, too.)
Lord, why couldn't it have been
Just one day later, then it would be the
Very first day of spring?
You see what I mean, God?

But the Lord gave me some blue today,
Thirty-some plus years later,
As I walked under cold winter's-end sky.
Celebrating return of my tiny purple crocuses
On the first day of the rest of my life.
Only passing through, you see.

Ice storm yesterday, couldn't stroll at all.
Today, frosty, but patched with azure sky, glimpses of
diamond sunrays peek out cheerily,
As if to greet me on this day.
Bird song despite all signs declaring it's still winter.
First robin of spring is busy,
He doesn't know how to grumble, he builds his nest,
He sings his sweet song
The Lord tells him to.

After yesterday's grumbledy-funk gloom of icy mess,
I decide to be happy today.
Even if—even if —things go downhill again,
Only passing through you see.
Father was merciful,
He "gave me some blue" today.

My Father's New Suit

My father wore an earth suit
Made of body, flesh and bone
But in an increment of time
Received new spirit and a heavenly home.

Daddy did not know the day
His outer tent he'd finally shed
But during his life's brief earthly stay
Believed that Christ died in his stead.

We all have died in Adam once
But still we get to make a choice
A life without the Lord of love
Or listen to the Spirit's voice.

Daddy chose to hearken
Believed in Christ when the Spirit called
Not knowing soon he'd shed his suit
God held him even during his fall.

My father fell down from a tree
Yet took the gift of Calvary
A suit of glory he now wears
While heavenly angels take pause and stare.

For Christ, Dad's Savior, took all his sin
Exchanged it for new life within
Now he's joined the heavenly throng
To sing God's praises in eternal song.

Just Who?

Who on earth do you think you are?
A voice screams loudly in my head.
Why put your thoughts down on a page?
For a world that's broken and dead.

Just what do you think you have to say
That hasn't been said before?
By someone much more loquacious than you
Go now, and please close the door.

Shamefully I went skulking along
The liar indeed had got his way
Thinking I had nothing fresh or new
Or even important to say.

But wait, a few words do still
Cry out from the pen of my soul
For there is no time to give up yet
Or to bury my words in a hole.

The thought that maybe there's someone
Who might need what I have to tell
Not any story from my broken life
But the words of Immanuel.

And so I keep plugging away
Trust Him to use words from my pen
If it helps one person to find Jesus Christ
I'd do it all over again.

Old Feet

I rub weakened legs with tiny ankles
and thickened fungal toes on petite aged feet,
with lotion, giving short lived comfort
to her old and weary feet.
Angry, flaking skin encompassing them,
Ready to be flung off
along with painful cracks and
rubbing toes.
Her beleaguered being is
plain tired with worn out feet.

Those feet were once
soft and pink and sweet.
Maybe tickled by her Mama?
Maybe played "This little piggy?"
Now ancient and weary from walking on
dreary paths on this death shadowed vale.
One day they will lay down to eternal rest.
One day her shoes will no longer be needed.
The cycle of life will march on
with younger, less callused feet.
Feet that have yet to earn their stripes,
that also will stumble many times along the path
in this mystery called life.

Her feet carried her through
times of war, poverty, anxiety,
and bogs of pain and sorrow.
At last, in one moment,
Suddenly fly, those feet will,
To velvety mansions above.
In an instant, they'll be
soft and cute and new again.
Eternally new tootsie toes
padding endlessly on streets paved with gold
in the New Jerusalem.
Never a callus or stubbed toe again.
Just beautiful, glorified feet.

A POTPOURRI OF PONDERINGS

Orange barn kitten in our Aunt Grace's yard in Jefferson, Iowa.

The Wandering Lamb

In vain I look around
Desperately seeking
Seeking someone from this world
Who would give me the kind of love You as You do.
There is no one, no one.

You're not surprised by this
For You look down in compassion, finding
That one of Your silly lambs
Has somehow left the flock again
Headed straight for the danger zone.

You reach for Your shepherd's crook
A crook made from trials, sicknesses
Tight places, even estrangements from loved ones.
In my extremity I feel the crook's tugging
Gently, then firmly pull me until I look to You again.

Even in discipline You're kind
Weighing out mercy for my misery.
Words of grace flow: No condemnation
Accepted in the Beloved, and Your promise:
"I will never leave you nor forsake you."

From the moment I was born
Cast from the womb to this merciless world
You were there – You were there.
You see me looking anxiously all around and say,
"Wandering lamb, come home."

Harmar Eagle

On barren branch he perches
Royal, majestic
Still a symbol
Of our broken
Once great land.

Below, unseeing drivers
Many holding shiny black lures
With messages that keep them
Earthbound
Face to the ground.
Oblivious.

They speed on by the hundreds
Cars parallel to the
Rough flow of muddy waters
Of the ancient Allegheny
Brackish water churns down to the city
The place called the Golden Triangle.

Mist is gently rising
From the day's incessant drizzle
From my seat in the car
I look for him each time I pass
Coming or going to the city
Or to visit mother, over the river
In the nursing home.

With eyes straining, I spot
Small shock of white feathers
That crowns his head, setting him apart.
"Hello, beautiful bird!" I shout.
So happy I feel, for
He's not a vulture
But our treasured national bird.
Blessed I am to see him there.

His nest he commandeered
From a hawk's, I heard
For that's what eagles do.
Two eaglets hatched this year
Still share the nest with him.

As a crazy, roaring
Interstate buzzes along below him.
Winding along a waterway.
He is unaware
Of the madness of our lives.
He sits as royalty,
Above it all
God's stately creature
Our beautiful bald eagle.

Hardened to Wonder

How is it that we get so hardened to wonder?
The miracle of a single breath,
The beating heart that never rests.

How is it that we don't take time to stop and consider?
Each snow crystal is unique,
Each human fingerprint also.

Here's a great mystery: Divine Knitting Needles.
They weave us in utter darkness
Inside our mother's womb.

Yet He knew every word we would say,
Every decision, right or wrong, we would make,
And yes, the blackness of our sins.

But because of His Son Jesus,
God's anger has been turned away.
And He has pardoned our ocean of iniquities.

Post-It Note to Self

Walk away from Facebook,
All the tweets on Twitter.
Put away the hearsay now,
And things that make me bitter.

Stop it with the selfies,
Instagram and Pinterest.
Instead, the Royal Son of God
He wants to be my interest.

Jesus Christ is waiting now,
While on His royal throne.
It's time for me to know Him now,
It's time to make Him known.

Stop looking at my blog stats,
And social media reading.
It's time to learn of Jesus now,
And on His Word be feeding.

"But these things are important!"
My flesh cries in protest
Oh self, stare up in the sky,
He'll soon be manifest!

And then this life, so pressing,
In an instant will be gone.
The One I was created for
His righteous reign will dawn.

Let Go the Chain

In a moment of time
The weight of one infraction
If I choose to cling to it
Will become my iron chain.

Then bondage comes
Decisions to hold grudges
Forever dividing families, friends.
Sorrows multiplying, paralyzing.

But with confession, release
His cleansing restores
Choose the Master's way above mine.
Girl, let go of your chain
Forgive.

Redeeming Time

How did this leaven enter my soul?
I, who thought I was wise.
Then, reading of those who went on before,
My lukewarm state I despise.

I thought I was rich,
But still am so poor,
When I look on my own barren heart.
And yet He still woos me,
And draws me near Him,
As ever, to have a new start.

Time is careening down history's hall,
Utter destruction since the day of man's fall.
And yet in a moment, I still can redeem,
To God and His Word reveal my esteem.

Time's nearly over,
My race nearly run.
I press on to finish,
What I have begun.

My life is worth nothing,
Except to know Him.
My gracious Redeemer,
And His victory win.

How Could it Be?

Black darkness, thicker
Than hell itself,
Surrounded to depths of very being.
My Lord sweating great drops of blood.

I was part of the great bruise,
Upon that sacred heel.
Weighed down with the world's sin
All too real.

And yet it stands
That it was His desire
To endure
Full punishment for me.

How could it be?
That He bore that full curse
So that I can from God's wrath
Be forever free?

Look Up

How His heart breaks
For those in darkness
Without a light to guide their way.

How His heart breaks
For those crushed under
Lies of sin they must obey.

Perchance, if they would
Look up to see His loving,
Waiting, outstretched arms.

They could find, as we did too
New hope and purpose.
No longer swayed by lying charms.

Creation is Crying

Pollen fuzzies
Dance in the unstable air
The birds are singing
But many dropping from the sky.
Sudden death, but how?
A mystery.
Everything blooming
Ahead of its time.
Floods, earthquakes, tsunamis, monsoons:
Everyday occurrences.
Creation knows
Something's up.
Violence covers the earth.
Days of Noah here once again.
Creation is crying
(Can you hear it?)
Pleading for Jesus to return
And heal this broken earth.
And He will
Sooner than we know.

Particles

The particles hang suspended
Between heaven and earth
A universe unto itself
Dust in motion
Slowly, deliberately
Pirouetting
Yet only seen through lens of light beam
Gliding, then disappearing
Into fabric of earth.

Man appears as budding flower
Then waltzes through life
Not knowing where he came from
Or why he's here
A speck of dust
His body on parade in
Some cosmic sphere
Arrested between light and darkness below.

If he perchance
Embraces the Source of light,
Of things unseen, beyond himself
Beyond his body – his very own
Man, made from dust particles
Will resurrect
Brand new sinless body
No longer consigned
To the earth dust from which he came.

Sudden Change

The cold weather swept in,
And with it gusted a cheerless day.
Welcome to the change in seasons,
Ready or not, here it comes,
Though I resisted its forceful call.
Gale-like November, drafts of gloom,
Leaves suddenly drop down, violent
Gravity plunges them toward grave of earth.
This world, the place where no man
Can revive his mortal soul.
A cold and lifeless sod.
Humors increasingly darkened,
Ice of winter looming ahead,
Though not welcomed here.
Yet shiver-chill incessantly pelts down,
With sleet of sorrow,
And unkind words
That cannot be unspoken.
Loneliness fills the darkened rooms of
The soul house deep inside.
Only comforts found
In Good Book
Which somehow thaws my frigid soul.
One tiny flicker of light from Him,
Imparts sheer glimpse of hope,
To go on one more day.

On Being Broken

His body was broken for us
And in His love, He breaks us too.
We, who wish to be like Him
Must also identify with His pain.

His body literally mangled
But ours – our pride in ourselves
Our need for acclaim, for man's applause
That's what needs to be broken in us.

If we are to share in His likeness
We must share in His sufferings too
Oh, but there is consolation
The Savior's unfailing love.

No matter what we're going through
Underneath – His everlasting arms
We sob, in grief in this rocky way
Through a vale of tears we call life.

But one day, grief will be gone forever
Peace and love and joy will remain
Dwelling with Him in eternal day
Pain of earthly past not even a thought.

For now, let us simply press on
Allow Him to take us through another day.
Be glad that He's seen fit to break us
Let His life, fine perfume,
Be poured out from within.

Turn Me

The world is losing its grip
I feel myself starting to slip
All alone in a big black world
Hell's lies are incessantly hurled
Hang on to what I know to be true
Hang on, it's all I can do.

The world has gone steadily crazy
And I've become spiritually lazy
In praying for the needs of lost man
Take time to, while I still can.
When it's easier, so easier, for me
Just sit back and turn on the TV.

The world's being sucked down to hell
Will I raise up my voice to tell?
To snatch others from hell's burning fire
For that is the cruel one's desire
For all men to join him there
An eternal and lifeless nightmare.

The onslaught is coming and here I just sit
With laissez faire thinking, so easy to quit
Waken my soul God, let me care for the lost
Be thou my vision as I count the cost
It seems so hopeless, but You are still there
Despite the world's darkness, I find You by prayer.

Soon all the memory of this world will fade
I'll join God's family in the heaven He made
Let life go on by then and live for the next
He promised to us His sweet peace and rest.
O turn me again, O Turner of hearts,
And once again I can make a fresh start.

When Confusion Comes In

When confusion comes in,
Does it come in slowly
An unwanted guest that sucks
Your thoughts and dreams and hopes
Like the dust that swirls in particles of sunlight
To a place far, far away?

A beautiful woman
A career minded man
Now reduced to shells
Their life now consisting
Of watching TV and picking up
Pieces of imaginary crumbs off
A dusty floor?

So very brief, this life
Our bodies fragile containers
Hold memories like unfinished
Cups of creamed coffee,
Cream leaves just a swirl where personality was.
Yet still the eyes will sometimes smile.

One solitary day
Does sense fly away?
You are there in the present
In one moment
And then you are gone
How does life soar away so fast?
Someone,
Please tell me.

My Work

In a world where men are striving,
To prove themselves, to build their name.
Hard work admired by so many,
Pull up your bootstraps, you'll get fame.

Jesus shared of a work of faith,
For those who've joined His family.
Not a labor of tough struggle,
God's work for us is to believe.

For faith's the one thing God requires,
Yet people urge sight evidence.
This planet's hostile to mere trust,
Man's gold standard is "common sense."

Was there sense when He hung dying?
His silence when they plucked His beard?
Soldiers laughing, the shame of spitting,
Yet faith says it's not what it appears.

Three days passed, this broken Savior,
Rose from the grave triumphantly.
And He held it not against us,
To His disciples, He said, "Peace."

He asks me simply to rest then,
Trust that He has good for me.
Until the day His face I see,
My work on earth is to believe.

Don't We All Need Jesus?

Don't we all need Jesus then
For every pain and tear
To run to Him and cling to Him
To chase away our fear?

Don't we all need Jesus then
When people let us down
Though we are only made of dust
For us He wore that crown.

Our sorrows borne in His body
When they nailed Him to the tree
Don't we all need Jesus then
To escape sin's tragedy.

Still

Even as
One's heart is breaking
There's still God's love
Free for man's taking.

Even when
All hope seems lost
Still there's the victory
Of the cross.

Even if many
Scoff at God's Word
Still good news of Jesus
Worldwide is heard.

Appearances deceive
Tell all kind of lies
Still hunger for meaning
Cannot be denied.

ABOUT THE AUTHOR

Megan E. Vance has been writing poetry since high school days and never can tell when a poem might pop into her head.

She has been married 35 years to her biggest supporter Kevin, is a mother to three, and grandmother to three.

In addition to writing, Megan enjoys reading the Bible, sewing, quilting, and treasures time with her "grandboys."

Megan is the author of a devotional book called *Sure Mercies: Hope for the Suffering*. (4RV Publishing, 2015)

She also has numerous written articles for magazines for children and for adults. Her work has been included in two anthologies by Tree Shadow Press: *Prompted Prodded Published: How Writing Prompts Can Help All Writers* (2016) and *Celebrate: A Collection of Life's Celebrations* (2019). She lives near Pittsburgh in Natrona Heights, Pennsylvania.

www.ingramcontent.com/pod-product-compliance
Lightning Source LLC
Chambersburg PA
CBHW031416040426
42444CB00005B/597